Universal Truths

Awakening to Enlightenment and Ascension

by

Philippe Roels

DEDICATION

I wish for all Seekers of Truth to find it in their hearts to be brave and
Honourable

Contents

ACKNOWLEDGMENTS

I would like to thank all the kind Beings that have assisted on my journey, Earth based and otherwise. I also want to thank my good friend Vania for her support and using the tools successfully. She has made massive progress herself as a result. Thank you also to Neena for the support during my darkest hours.

Prologue

"The urge to discover the truth that completes you!"

This urge has taken many forms in the last few years, many people have been looking for a method to reach Within themselves. At first, this was not an obvious change, it appeared to be an ordinary shift in life as life does. When I look back, I can see the path I took and the reasons for my choices. I am referring to my personal journey, but I am sure it is like the journey of many others.

"The System" is a set of tools or keys I found to be crucial in my development. Without these tools as foundations I would not have made any progress. These tools help unlock new avenues otherwise invisible to you.

I wrote this book to share information discovered whilst searching for Universal Knowledge. I found this information to be key in facilitating many discoveries. Many trials and experiences enabled me to make good progress and discover tremendous things on this path.

I hope this will inspire you too.

Philippe Roels

Introduction

"You have not lived until you almost died and for those that have experienced this, life has a flavour the protected will never know!"

I remember the first time I read this statement. It made such an impact on me, and thirty-five years later it is still fresh in my mind. I have experienced this kind of situation myself, it rings true for me. Little did I realise, it would happen several times in my life. I was humbled by the awesome power of the ocean and the beautiful sky has taken me to the edge of fear but most dangerous has been the uncompromising, selfish arrogance of man. Mankind remains the most unpredictable and to this day I am still surprised by the level of fear acted out.

It saddens me to find, Man still behaving from a basic instinct point of view, filled with fear and fighting with his fellow man. Someone once quoted "Man's inhumanity to Man", so true. Man, in his fall from grace has forgotten about being united as a species. This perceived separation perpetuated by religions has caused heartache and anguish on many levels. It has however, provided us with the experience, we as Universal beings, crave. This physical experience has been the Soul's playground but Man's jail. The road of enlightenment is not an easy one. It takes many lifetimes to arrive on this final path. I say the road of enlightenment because it is not a destination but a journey. Enlightenment is a process of discovery and it is ongoing until you ascend. Death, believed to be the ultimate peril by man, is in fact not a peril. It is a process and a necessary one. One's life has to end to grow and evolve or we would remain stationery in a particular phase. Most people are reluctant to change their circumstances and therefore growth is finite for them. A person will only change their beliefs and core philosophies when they fail and no longer serve them. This is quite an extreme situation, but it happens. A lot has to do with the Soul's chosen path for the current incarnation and this seldom changes during a lifetime, but it does with a new life or incarnation. Man is by default a creature of habit because routine is safety, it's predictable and would appear to be more controllable. This ability to control one's environment gives Man security and comfort. Man's basic nature functions on this planet by using numeric algorithms. Language functions by recognising the repeated sequence of letters and if you remove the odd letter here and there, the language still works. The sequence and positioning of the letters make it recognisable. The processing power of the mind analyses the structure. If the equations make sense or do not change, then man feels safe. It's part of the survival instinct and is very primal. If the sequence changes then fear sets in. Any unusual number sequence is met with a fear-based reaction resulting in fight or flight. It is all designed for survival of the species.

As we gain experience during our many life times, we cannot help but grow wiser and all aspects are "Owned" following the experiences. The path of the Soul is such that eventually experiences are no longer required. Further growth does not happen and there are no longer any benefits to incarnating here in this dimension. At this point Souls choose to incarnate to help others.

There is a shift in frequency in the local space density right now and this allows a Soul to connect with its Higher Self easier than previously. Due to the increase in frequency or decrease in density, depending on which way you look at it, a Soul is separated from its Higher Self. Now it can connect as if it has bridged the gap. The only way to achieve this is to raise the frequency of your Aura or incarnated Soul. Once you reach a certain frequency, then contact and communication is possible, two become one in this time a space. Knowledge is no longer restricted, and the veil has disappeared. This process is Ascension but before you can ascend, you need to become enlightened to this process. If you fail to travel the road of Enlightenment, then you will not discover the knowledge to ascend. Enlightenment is being aware of yourself as not being confined to this time and place. Being aware of the fact you are not separate from your Higher Self. It is the wish to reach for communion with the higher Self and to become the higher Self. This is the feeling you will have when it happens to you. You find that information beyond this time and space arrives to you. It's an awakening, a waking up to the fact you have been asleep and restricted. Most people go on about daily life not considering the fact that this dimension is an illusion. It is a creation to enable the experience of a concept. Left and right exist in this dimension as two separate places. Left and right are connected by a third place and that is the space between them. This is the basic design of this dimension but outside this dimension or illusion, left and right exist as one space or place, they are a unit. They are not separate and only in this dimension can you experience these aspects as separate entities or places.

On becoming Awakened the real work starts because responsibility increases. This taking of responsibility is a requirement to become Enlightened. You come to realise that decisions you take have consequences. These decisions will lead to uncovering a path. The path will adjust dynamically as you make the decisions. After being on the path for some time, you will see the results of your choices as it changes your reality almost instantly. It is quite something to observe as it happens, and it empowers you further. For some it is still not enough of a wake-up call and they continue to ignore the push or need to "Live in Truth". Living in Truth is vital, or progress will stall. Some experience a great deal of physical pain as the Aura tries to morph to higher frequencies. The pain experienced is energy that is locked in place and cannot flow. Energy needs to flow at all times, like a river. This pain experienced, can and has caused some to turn away from the path, the pain disappears but so does your progress. If you listen and become sensitive to your own energy, then you will be guided by the Higher Self on how to change. The early symptoms will be audible frequency sounds appearing in and around you. You will also feel an invisible force almost like a magnetic field in your Aura and physical body. This can cause a change in temperature and tingling sensations like pins and needles. The road of enlightenment is hard and requires self-discipline. There are many scary moments filled with self-doubt and it is not for the faint hearted. The good news is that movement brings change and if you work on yourself, then movement happens, and change comes. There are also many moments of pure bliss and ultimate peace. Many insights follow, and Universal knowledge arrives.

The Christians speak of the pearly gates with Saint Peter and the Egyptians speak of balancing the scales of Maat with Anubis. This highlights that before proceeding on ascension you had to be pure of heart. Even though you might be an Enlightened being your choices have consequences and poor choices halt your progress. An Enlightened soul can still make poor choices and lose the privilege of ascension, but this is unlikely to happen to a Soul as its path is part of the experience. It is a conscious decision to live in Truth or not to. If you do not choose Truth, then you will live in fear and this will cause your frequency to remain lower than required to ascend. Living in fear is a third dimensional experience and so you will remain within this dimension if you choose to hang on to fear. From personal experience I suggest that you obtain guidance and support during this trying time as it is easy to doubt yourself. An experienced person can reassure you and confirm where you are in your development. Today there is no need to die to reach the pearly gates or balance the scales of Maat. Conscious Enlightenment and Ascension happens whilst you are alive. It all depends on the soul's chosen path but if you are reading this, then you are already well on your way on this path. This is the magic of the current times as you can Atone and ascend whilst conscious, you are the judge and the jury of yourself. It's not complicated, but it helps to have insight, and this is the reason for this book.

Looking around, I can see that the urge to search for this knowledge has happened to many people. I was expecting it to be a larger percentage of the population by now. I hazard a guess that the numbers are in the thousands not millions at this point. The current situation will offer many changes in all walks of life. As I observe my peers in my small area of influence, I can see there are a few people involved in the changes. Alarming for me is that those engaged on the path of Enlightenment miss details and still struggle with aspects of Fear based realities. We understand this concept of fear, but it traps us within the Ego experience. We use the Ego to navigate and research our salvation and this puts us at a disadvantage. It is like trying to repair a car with substandard tools.

The greatest issue is that without knowing, we are seeking enlightenment using the Ego, but the Ego needs to be transcended to evolve and ascend. So, we have a problem and it would appear that this could lead us into a cycle or loop. Even more confusing is that when we contemplate this it feels as if it traps us. This can perpetuate and drive you round the bend should you choose let it.

If you understand this, then you have already arrived at a place with answers. This is the point where I remind you that you are not alone, and you never were. I'm not talking about family, friends or any human company, I'm talking about your Higher Self. This is where it gets funky and science fiction "like", where reality crashes into the illusion and makes a big bang. Where you wake up to the fact that this has all been a dream. The person you think you are is in fact NOT you. It is just a vehicle, like your car to get to and from work. Your body, your environment, this reality IS NOT. It's a creation to help you but no longer serves you and the funny thing is, you can feel this. We all can, hence the frantic search and questioning you are experiencing, something is wrong, and you can't quite put your finger on it. You can feel this in the background as a subtle calling.

The urge…. the pull, it's getting stronger.

You might think, What do I do? How???

You might try Meditation in various forms, Tai Chi and Yoga. At the onset it feels great, you have found solace, a method to fill the void. It's hard this new lifestyle, you are desperate to get ahead, and you want to become proficient. The Ego shouts out in fear of change and tells you to go to the pub for a drink, "We can go to Yoga next week". It is very hard to be strong and stay focused as there are many distractions. If you are in a relationship where you are not both searching for answers, then this can be hard too. I know, because I have been there. This is where it gets tough, but I can tell you with the utmost certainty, if you trust your feelings then you will see your truth and, in that moment, you will know.

Do not ignore these experiences and feelings! As these are the early revelations, the training ground. If you notice experiences like this and are aware that they are happening to you...... then you have arrived at the start of the end game. If you are aware of such occurrences, then it's time to explore "why?" in all of this.

You have gained awareness. Think about it for a moment....! This is a huge step.

You have been "Upgraded" to an aware state of being. You are "Awakened" and have been "Enlightened". The light of your Higher Self is shining on you like a spot light.

There is only one catch at this point but if you are in the habit of living your life within Truth, then you have nothing to worry about. Being aware of your awakening, you now have the responsibility of choice. Be very careful with integrity, both yours and others. This will become clearer when we discuss achieving balance or clearing Karma as it's known in some circles. I try very hard to stay non-denominational when it comes to a religious text as this is the product of Ego. All have valuable lessons in various areas, but we need to accept that it's a construct of this reality. I say it in this manner to use a point of reference to measure or for comparison as we need to set a baseline to work from.

When I talk about reality, then I like to think of it from the Higher Self perspective and the Ego perspective as the illusion. The reason for this is that we are moving towards erasing the Ego and becoming the Higher Self. So, everything to do with the Ego will go, fear and such too.

Right! So, we know a few things but most stay elusive and we are still not sure about the validity of others. So how do we work it out? What is

Truth and what is not? Whom has the authority to tell if it's right or wrong? Is the Universe real? Can you can change your current reality?

Questions… many questions!

Would you like to know a secret? You!….. You are the one with all the answers to your questions.

So how do we get the answers? So how do we connect to our higher Selves? How do I get rid of Fear?

The following tools are techniques I used to forge my path and with 20 years of experience I have seen many options. This does not mean I have all the answers, but I can share my experiences and hopefully some will assist you with your quest.

I have seen many things from this world and others. I have experienced invisible forces from this world and beyond. I fought Fear, some people might refer to this as evil. This personal quest has exposed me to tremendous pain and heartache but there were moments of limitless Love and peace that reaches beyond this Universe. I have seen and experienced both sides of the scales on the range of emotion and always pushed for the greatest experience. All the while remaining true to myself even to my detriment at times. It's been a hard ride, but it's paid off. Always BE honourable, the primary aim.

Let's begin!

Meditation

Well, meditation is a key element and I consider it the foundation for all development work

Let us consider two features or specific aspects of meditation. There are many facets to meditation and each facet will suit people at various points in their lives. Once you master the essentials, it is possible to modify this practice to your own desires and for most individuals this takes place without realising it. One form that has become established as mindfulness is an excellent place to commence as it is basic, and you can use it anywhere. The technique involves observing an aspect of what is taking place in your life. This could be a thought or feeling and you can use this as a focal point to calm yourself and relax into a comfortable peace. I should add at this point that the primary purpose of meditation is to "switch off" the noisy outside world and allowing yourself to "hear" the inner still voice. The mindfulness technique is a good one to start with. If you have never delved into the meditation before start with mindfulness. However, this is not the object of this book and I believe if you are reading this information then you are beyond this level of meditation. I have not aimed this information at beginners, but should you require advice about mindfulness, you are welcome to contact me to discuss. The technique I will discuss has become the most useful one for myself and the main reason for this is because it's basic and can be used with great success. It can be adjusted to suit personal needs, and that's the point, simple but effective. I have used this technique in my deepest and darkest moment of development when everything else failed to arrive to my rescue. Let me explain a little more and you will understand.

Imagine that you are in a massive storm out at sea being tossed around like a champagne cork with nowhere to cling to. Now also imagine besides this, the level of fear you are experiencing due to those circumstances. As far as you can perceive, there is no safety anywhere and the possibility of rescue does not exist.

Although this may sound scary and something you would like to avoid, it is not traumatic. I am trying to paint a picture to show how hard it was to maintain focus when the force of the Universe arrived and coursed through me. It was overwhelming as I had never experienced this level of energy before. As a result, my level of fear was elevated a great deal. At this point of my journey I was dealing with shedding of fear as the last bastion on becoming the master of my emotions. The only platform to cling to was this technique and the rest of reality became a blur, disappearing as if torn up by a tornado. I could sense fear arriving in the distance and closing in on me with determination and purpose. It felt like I was in a dark forest and hundreds of red eyes appeared all around me. They were closing in on me, the wolves were close. This was fear, but I remained calm with the use of this technique. I kept fear at bay and even forced its retreat and turned the situation around. I settled down and could experience the full force of the energies flowing through me. It was amazing, I lay there on my Yoga mat for hours or, so it seemed.

After that experience, I realised that there was no reason for any other method of meditation.

I have stayed with this ever since and use it to traverse through the meditative state into Allowance and to a much deeper level I like to call "Surrender". Once at the level of Surrender, meditation becomes more of an observation than a meditation. I will explain this in depth later.

let us examine the ingredients of this technique and its use.

It involves breathing in through the nose and breathing out down towards the base of the spine. Sounds simple, and it is. I like to call this technique as "The breath"

This can be adapted to suit yourself but for now let us look at my method in more detail.

Find yourself a comfortable position, I guess either sitting or lying down. I am sure you have enough experience by now to know what is best for you.

Now, take a few moments just to relax and notice your body position and environment. Be aware of the sounds around you and their location in relation to you.

Pay attention to your normal breathing pattern and the route the air takes. The "In and Out" of breath. Picture the path of your breath, in and out. Do this for a minute or two. Take note relaxation arriving but remember at this stage you are not doing anything. All you are doing is just breathing and paying attention to this process.

After a few minutes you can adjust the breathing.

At this point we can create a mental picture of your breath being split into two parts. The "in breath" and the "out breath". Both the "In" and "Out" breath need to be measured using time. The "in breath" will be shorter than the "out breath". The best way to visualise this is to imagine that you are breathing through your nose towards the back of your head. Try to see the distance from your nose to the back of your head as the time that the "in breath" lasts. Imagine the air travelling inside a tube from the tip of your nose to the back of your head. Now as you breathe out, direct the air towards the base of your spine. When you transition from the "in" to "out" breath you can visualise the air making a semi-circle to find its way into the tube that travels down the spine. Remember that the "out breath" should last until you reach the base of the spine. It will take practice to work-out the timing for yourself as we are different and have different lung capacities. Again, use the glass tube to help with the visualisation and direct the air down this tube. Imagine your spine is made of glass and use that image.

Continue with this exercise until you relax down. You can use this for many reasons and a great tool to have as you will discover on your path.

At first it may feel a little awkward but stick with it even if it requires 10 minutes or more. As we are all different, the time involved will vary but keep practising and experiment with variations.

It is an easy focus that requires little effort to carry out as breathing is natural by default.

Once you are happy with this process, then it's time to raise the level for added benefit. Remember that the driving factor here is "Intention" and this will be the theme throughout this book.

Using this method gives you the freedom of observation. This means you are free to notice changes within your Aura and any incoming energy will be noticeable to you.

We can expand to the next step using the same technique but now as you reach the bottom of the "Out breath" you take a slight pause. With this slight pause lasting up to 2 seconds, allow yourself to stop before taking the "in breath" again and in that small space push downwards into the perineum as if trying to push your intention out through the space below your spine. It's only a slight push, gently, then once again breathe in. Continue this further.

The last step with this tool is attaching "Intention" with each phase of "The breath".

There are three phases to the technique. The "In breath", the out breath and the pause in between. During the "in breath" think positive thoughts like, why you are doing this process. During the "Out breath" simply, Allow. During the pause at the end, Surrender.

In breath: Visualise the distance to the back of your head and see the breath travel as you breathe in.

Feel the texture of the air or even see it as energy instead.

Remember "Intention" is the key here.

Out breath: Visualise your spine as a glass tube and allow the breath to fall down the length of the tube.

Feel the texture of the air or even see it as energy instead.

Remember that "Allowance" is key here. You are allowing this to happen, giving yourself permission. It might be important for you to contemplate what this means to you beforehand.

The pause: Visualise the act of pushing down at the base of your spine as if you are pushing the air through the skin.

It needs to feel as if you are "giving up" on everything, even life. This is about total Surrender, a complete release and letting go.

Remember Surrender is key here. Again, contemplate what this means to you beforehand as it may help you.

Energy Work

Energy is a wonderful thing and presents itself in many forms.

We as humans have a set of guidelines or expectations for identifying energy and we rely on experience in our early lives to recognise it.

Depending on your experience, your knowledge about energy will vary. The most commonly experienced are in two distinct areas. These are pressure or temperature related.

So, what do I mean in this case, well with pressure it could feel like an increase or decrease in weight. This can be felt with various parts of the body. The most common parts of the body to sense changes in pressure are with the head or the hands. The ability to sense an increase in pressure will alert you to a change but by the time you sense it at this level, the change is already marked. This has been happening for some time because subtle changes are more difficult to recognise at first. The more you work with energy, the easier it is to notice finer changes.

The same applies to temperature variations. A variation in energy can be due to change in the type or level of energy. Energy is uniform by nature like the atmosphere or the ocean, but it can be manipulated. The changes occurring will be what you can sense. Also, as we are individuals, these fluctuations are interpreted differently. To one person it may be cold but hot to another.

The movement or Flow of energy can feel like a magnetic wave or a variation in pressure localised in a small space. This is the most common way to recognise the "Flow" of energy. The energy could feel as if you are holding two magnets that are interacting either by pushing or pulling but this invisible force is the best comparison. One last common sensation is tingling in hands or limbs. This can occur if the Flow is restricted somehow. This can also happen when the Flow is interrupted instead of being uniform.

I am sure that with your level of experience you can identify with most of the descriptions. The Aura can be used as a sensory tool, it is the Soul in this dimension. The more we practice, the better we can use this as a tool in the same way we use our physical body to interact in this world. To do this, we need to explore the Aura and become familiar with it. There are many methods to explore the Aura. This is a large topic on its own and I will not be elaborating on it in this book. I suspect you will have this basic knowledge already. We do however need insight about the interaction of energy and how it interacts with the Aura itself. We need to experience this happening and be fluent in identifying external stimuli when it happens. This is crucial for you, being able to identify the Higher Self and understanding information that is being relayed to you. The information will arrive as energy and penetrate the Aura. You will recognise this event happening and sense the change in levels of energy. Frequently information will be contained within the energy. This is one method of providing you with information. If you cannot translate from energy to intelligent information, you will miss the message. So, you can see how important it is to develop this skill.

You will need to develop sensitivity to energy and there is no substitute for experience in this case. Even limited experience is better than nothing. You can build on this and you can do this by setting your "Intention" for this purpose. The easiest method is to set aside some time for yourself and choose a location where you have space to move. A space 2 by 2 metre should do to start with and if you have a Yoga mat, use that. The idea is to start a training schedule for "Moving Meditation" as this will lead to communication with your Higher Self. If you practice Yoga or Tai Chi, you will have a good foundation. This will be crucial to your development once you are working with your Higher Self as you will move together as a unit. Developing a relationship with your Higher Self is the goal as together you will continue further on the Enlightenment path. You will need to spend time on the mat to develop the relationship. At this point you will combine what you have learned so far. This will include Meditation, the breath and energy work.

Progress may appear to be slow at first, but the most important thing is to arrive on the mat each time. Even if it appears that you are not making progress, make the effort. Your Intention has to be such that you are determined to make time for yourself on the mat. Even if you sit on the mat and do nothing. At least be present as this is part of the creative process in your path going forward. This is VERY important! Your mat has to become your sacred place. In the beginning it will be difficult to make time but as you progress, things will change and later it will be difficult NOT to arrive on the mat.

Awakening to Enlightenment and Ascension

Moving Meditation

Even if you practice Yoga simply stand on the mat and be still. There is no need to do any Yoga at this stage.

Start small and over time add extra components to your practice. Begin with your feet hip distance apart, relaxed and simply breathe. Have your arms hanging at your sides with your shoulders relaxed. Practice "The Breath" or be still and observe. Feel and sense where you are. Notice subtle things happening to you and around you. Once relaxed, you can hold your hands out in front of you, not high up but as if you are receiving something from someone, about waist height is good. Now picture the Sun shining down into your hands and see what happens. The most important aspect at this phase is "Trust". You need to trust the process and yourself. What I mean by this is that you need to believe you are worthy for this to happen for you. The more you practice the easier it will become as you will be able to observe the changes and see the results. It does not appear as if you are doing any work but in fact you are and it's very subtle. You are now working on a different level than you are used to and therefore the results will not be as you would usually expect. It will take a little time to notice the change and also depend on how sensitive you are when it comes to energy work. Again, I remind you, we are all different and results will vary. The only way is to stay focused and continue to present yourself on the mat.

At some point you will feel energy and when this happens then you need to just allow this to take place. There are a few things that you can pay attention to at this stage. You will experience what appears to be something like pressure changes. Let me give you an example. Imagine for a moment you have two magnets, one in each hand. As you bring the magnets closer together they start to interact. If you move them extremely slowly, then you will feel the change in the magnetic force happen gradually. So now imagine that you have them at a point where they just start to react to each other, only a little. At this point you would stop moving them towards each other but now instead, move them from side to side. Ensure that the distance of the magnets from each other remains constant. You will feel the direction of the force change but not reduce in strength. Can you picture this scenario? If you can't then I suggest that you get hold of some magnets and try this as it is important that you understand this aspect. It will be imperative to understand this as these pressure changes will be the guidance to movement in a particular direction. I'm talking about your body movement. For example, if you feel a pressure on the right side of your hand, it will be trying to move it towards the left. To accompany this sensation, you might feel the need to move in a specific direction and this is a good thing. It's called guidance and you need to listen to these feelings. This is where trust becomes important because if you trust then you will believe the feeling that accompanies it and act accordingly.

At first this will feel a little odd but a combination of Allowing and Surrendering will bring results.

There will be a multitude of emotions and feelings involved coupled with sensations relating to energy flow. Mostly it will be about testing this level of communication and finding what works for you. Nobody can advise you on how to respond as it is something that is as personal as the way you walk and talk. The description you have here is how I found this to work for myself, but it is difficult to relay all the aspects and there is no right or wrong way. There is only one requirement, and that is you need to turn up for this to happen. Keep practising and trust your feelings. If you are practising with this technique, then in no time you will experience the energy build up when you conduct the usual Yoga practice. This happened to me and then it was a case of exploring and understanding what was happening. As you allow this process to happen your trust will grow and it will feel like you are connecting, and results will occur. This is a huge confidence builder and will drive you to explore further. For me it was a case of surrendering to the process and allowing my Higher Self to take control of my body. Soon I was being guided and adjusted into some crazy Yoga positions. All this time trusting the process and therefore trusting my Higher Self. This took me into a non-standard Yoga practice and I often wondered if I was doing the correct thing. It was very hard to depart from the standard Yoga sequences and postures and my ability to trust was put to the test further. Did I really trust my Higher Self? Did I trust the path I could not see? Did I trust that my Higher Self knew my body better than I did and therefore knew how I needed to progress further? Could I Allow this to happen by Surrendering to it? These were the tests and believe me, your depth of character is tested, your integrity, your core and most of all - are you still fearful?

Make time for yourself, arrive on the mat and allow the force of the energy to push you into movement. The rest will come to you.

Philippe Roels

Face the Mirror

There are parameters that need to be examined to harness their full potential.

The first one is Trust and without this you have no chance of success. This does sounds harsh but there is no other way. If you cannot trust others, you therefore cannot be trusted either, there is no point to carry on any further. You need to change this within yourself before going further. Without trust you cannot believe the incoming information and end up going in the wrong direction. The good news is that you will know this and need to be honest with yourself to capitalise on this. The way to achieve this is by using a technique I like to call "Facing the mirror". This is something I developed myself and found that it is a good foundation to work from. The reason is you need a clean slate to start from. Imagine for a moment to trying to find one item on a floor covered in other items. The unwanted items will hinder your progress, delay you or even prevent you from finding that special item you need. Firstly, to achieve this we need to examine the items on the floor and get rid of the ones not required. This will help us lighten the workload when searching. Secondly, we need to be familiar with the remaining items and know them well so that when something new is introduced, we will notice this straight away.

So that is the basic principle and if we apply this to ourselves, then it will be as follows.

When you look into the mirror, I suggest that you physically do this as it will help you intimidate yourself into being honest, sounds comical but it works. So, my challenge to you is "Can you face yourself in the mirror?" Think about this and again if you cannot do this then it's a non-starter. The good news is that it does not matter to anybody but yourself. Nobody needs to know the contents of your exercise when you face the mirror. This is a personal dialogue and designed for you to make progress. To discover who YOU are at a level you are not used to working at. This is important! I cannot emphasise this enough as you need to know your good points and bad points. If you don't like the bad points, then you can change them. If you can live with them, then carry on as you are. You will "feel" if this is the correct way to progress or not. If you do not want to change but feel deep down somewhere that you should then you already know the answer, don't you? Listen…. feel and learn. This is the discovery of the Self so why deny yourself the experience and lose the benefit from this experience. Don't get me wrong this is not easy BUT…. How serious are you about progress? The choice is yours, nobody is asking you to do this and to be honest nobody cares what you choose. This decision will impact nobody else but you. I don't mind what your choice is, and you can walk away. Many have walked away before because this is not for everyone. Thinking you are ready is not the same as knowing you are ready.

This is the famous judgement we have heard about, but nobody ever told you that you would be the judge. They never told you that there would be no damnation and no retribution. You choose what you deserve for your actions and nobody needs to know. So, can you do it? Can you look into the mirror and admit to yourself, who you are? This is where the truth will set you free. The factor that limits people from doing this are the lies and the fear of being found out. Conditional Love also known as judgement lurks overhead generating disproportionate levels of fear. Once you launch yourself down this path and take up this challenge, then you will shed a huge load from your shoulders. You will be free and a step closer to shedding fear. So, step up to the mirror and reveal the truth, reveal the real you. Be kind to yourself and gift yourself this option. Being judged by their peers is one of man's greatest fears as they believe it leads to discrimination and separation form the group. Unfortunately, from experience it usually does. Most unenlightened people look for ways to feel better about themselves. They do this by finding somebody in a worse situation than themselves and comparing. These people might create a situation to put others down too. They end up believing that they have gained the upper hand. This is an illusion. Here, there is no need for this fear as it is a personal dialogue, and nobody needs to know if you feel less worthy or not. Self-worth or Self-love is lacking in each of these instances and part of the enlightenment process is finding this self-worth. We can only do this by confronting fear and seeing that we are worthy. This is the target to aim for and how soon you arrive here is up to you.

Peel the Onion

This a technique to examine fear-based experiences.

We remove the pain associated and so dispel the fear controlling this experience.

You can use this tool along with "Facing the mirror", discussed in the earlier chapter. Fearful events known as trauma are a common theme for humans in this life and take many forms. These range from physical to emotional trauma and produce challenges in our experiences. We need to dispel the fear to release the pain contained within the experience. This may sound odd, but these fear-filled experiences cause imbalance hence the pain. The pain is because of judgement on behalf of the person within the experience. Let me give you an example to highlight this.

Let's say in our example you were a victim of abuse as a child and this experience has caused you emotional trauma. Now as an adult realise that it's time to face this head on. Perhaps you had counselling for this in the past, but this does not guarantee that the pain has been removed from the experience. The only way to know is to observe how you feel about an event.

This stage is crucial, and you need to exercise truth to ensure a clean break from this. There is no hiding place from this truth and once again, you will know. This personal examination will not affect anybody but yourself. Be honest and work with it.

Now we look into the mirror and come to some conclusions about our personal reality. Pain is still present and associated with the abusive experience in earlier life. At this point you can take the experience as a single event. You can examine this event yourself as long as you use the fundamental basics based in truth. The best is method is to sit in Meditation, observe the event and ask questions.

Picture the event as if it was an onion made up of many layers. The object is to reach the centre that contains the truth. Once you find the truth, the pain associated with the event will disappear. All you need to do is assign blame to the party responsible. What remains is the experience. This experience will appear only as a series of images to remind you, but it will no longer hurt you by causing an emotional reaction.

This is important for your growth because you will need to become master of your emotions instead of being a slave to them. You can experience the emotions but not be hurt by them. You will act instead of re-acting. This is good training for you as you will use this further along the road in your quest for personal development.

To start the exercise, you can sit in Meditation and get yourself into a relaxed state. When you are ready bring forth an image or first thought relating to the traumatic event. Whilst examining the event you are searching for the place to attach responsibility. This is relevant when dealing with trauma. Look for the one responsible for creating the event that resulted in your pain. There are always two parties involved and, in this case, the victim and the abuser. Remember this is only an example to illustrate this tool.

You may think it will be obvious finding which is which when it comes to a victim or abuser. What you have to remember is that many abusers convince the victim that they are responsible at some level. This is often the reason this never gets resolved. In this example, a child will always be the victim no matter what reason the adult will have. The adult will always set the example as they have more experience in this world. Responsibility can be attributed in this case and the adult has to accept this. Once the child can see this for themselves, then the burden of responsibility disappears, and the pain is gone. It will be ideal if the victim can confront the abuser. Explaining to the abuser that they need to take ownership of the imbalance caused. They created the situation resulting in pain and emotional distress.

The process requires that we question the events. We can ask questions like "Why" this took place and "Who" created the situation. These are powerful questions. In turn the answers to those particular questions can be examined or dissected. Further questions can arise as a result. In this way we drill down into the event and reveal the ultimate truth or "Core Intention" at the heart of the event. For example, if the abuser was abused themselves then who is to blame. If we know the current abuser, then we can drill down into their experience by "Peeling the onion" and using the questions. Eventually we may arrive at the root or core. This is not necessary as we are all responsible for ourselves. In this instance there is no need, but it could be done. You could examine the abuser's life too.

At each layer or level once you have asked the questions you can either pass responsibility to the other party or take ownership yourself. You can then continue down to the next level. Continue with the process until one party clearly has the responsibility. If it belongs to you, then you have choices. You can release it or carry the burden. If the responsibility belongs to someone else, then you are free and can let go. If the responsibility belongs to the other party, then you can write a letter to them explaining how you feel. You do not need to post it but the act of writing it does the required work for you and the pain is released.

I realise that this is difficult and if you need help, then get in touch.

I can be contacted via my website www.universaltruths.co.uk on email: info@univesraltruths.co.uk

Face Fear

This is quite tough to do depending on where you are in your life.

For myself the turning point with this concept, because I have no other name for it, was to arrive at the realisation that we cannot die. Although this sounds simple and today most people are not strangers to this concept, it's quite something else to integrate this into your life and make it part of your reality.

I often say to people, "What's the worst thing that can happen in your life?... You die!...... and? what's the problem? You will die anyway, so why worry?" Why concern yourself with something as small as fear when there are bigger things to worry about? So, when you think along those lines then fear is not a great issue. Another way to approach this is, "if others can face fear then I can too!" Think yourself as invincible. See all this as a test, this life. It's a movie and you're only an actor playing a part but soon the film ends, and you arrive back in reality. Think bigger, think travelling the Universe is where you belong, and you're being restricted by being here on Earth. I think it makes things more "Real", this feeling of being part of the Universe. Especially when you can feel unseen forces around your body. You accept that there is more to this than just going to work each day. You feel as if you're a part of the Universe, almost as if you have become part of the "inner Circle" of information about how the Universe works and how it's made up. Suddenly you are aware of your own energy, you're in the game and you feel more connected with this added responsibility.

The secret to gaining inner strength is to face fear. You find the drive to search for more within the Universe. You realise that there is so much more to discover. You choose to face fears in order to make more progress. It's an exciting time.

Tackling fear can be scary or it can be a challenge. The choice lies with the individual and I think the motivating factor will be how you want to get ahead. To help yourself cope, you can try to view fear as energy that does not belong within your Aura. Another method you can use is to just surrender to it and observe. This makes it a more of an objective exercise as you are able to distance yourself from the emotion. Do this a few times and you will begin to realise that fear is powerless. It is only as powerful as you make it. The simplest way to combat fear is to remain calm and be at peace. To help in this endeavour, you can use "The Breath". As you observe fear starting to arrive, you may choose to breathe it back down and Allow this to happen. It's at times like these that you come to realise how much you create of your own reality. Once you see the fear retreat as a result of your efforts then you arrive at this conclusion. Of course, there are many levels of fear and some are well hidden or disguised. This is a journey of discovery and once you realise that you have control of fear then you arrive in a powerful position. You are no longer controlled by fear and tremendous freedom arrives. The method you have used to overcome fear becomes a sacred tool to yourself and you move forward on your path once more with added confidence.

To examine the feeling known as fear we need to look at a very subtle level. You will observe a change in energy within your Aura. This will happen around the Solar plexus area. That feeling that has been labelled as "Your gut instinct", the one that warns you about something not feeling right. We all know this feeling and it can sometimes present as a nauseating background feeling. A little like when you start to feel hungry, it's the same place and has to do with the interaction of the energy within the local Chakra. You can now see why it's imperative to be in touch with your own energy, to understand your Aura and to know the difference between your energy and energy originating outside yourself. The Solar plexus Chakra is the centre of personal power. If this energy centre is balanced, then you project a confident presence that allows you to navigate this world without fear. This should not be compared to having a large Ego. It most certainly is not that at all. It is a quiet strength that need not be displayed. It is a strength that radiates from you with no action required and people around you will notice this. As the disruptive feeling arises, you can make a conscious choice to move this up and out through your throat Chakra. Take your time and visualise this energy that is disturbing your peace and move it upwards. Move it through your chest and up to your throat. Once in the throat area, breathe this out of the local throat Chakra. Imagine that you are breathing out through your throat and not your nose or mouth. Continue to do this several times until the disturbance in the solar plexus disappears, or the fear disappears. Peaceful feelings will return to your heart. Remember it's about Intention.

As you tackle these occurrences, the energy within your Aura will adjust and clear. You will feel lighter as this burden of energy is lifted. Know that moving this energy can and most of the time will cause an emotional reaction. This is normal and part of the process. This has to happen in order for you to transmute the energy into something that will enable your aura to resonate at a higher frequency. For this to happen, the old lower frequency energy has to be "Shifted or transmuted" it has to be changed as

31

it no longer serves you. You will feel strong feelings arrive into either your chest or throat and it is very IMPORTANT that you do not suppress this process otherwise you are undoing all your hard work and you will need to go through this process again. Breathe this out and allow the feelings to surface and leave your body. Do this once but do it properly. Do not mess around with uncertainties here. You need understand that your body is reacting to the flow of energy and it is showing you what is happening. You need to observe this and understand this. If you feel the need to cry, then go ahead and "Allow" this to take place. You are now working on a different level. You are "Awakened" and must face these trials if you are to progress. Fear WILL try to stop you. You must be prepared for this and spot it when it happens. Be strong and allow the feelings to arrive and move you, they will arrive, and they will pass. Only then will you evolve and become master of your emotions. Becoming master of your emotions leads to an unfamiliar place. I found myself trying to reach for the meditative state as I had done in the past. For some reason I could not find it but after a time I found the answer. I was now in a different state of being and I no longer needed to travel to the meditative state as I was already there. This kind of shift happens often when you work on this path. It's exciting and new discoveries await all the time. So, dive into the fire, the deeper you go the better you will clear all this out and the faster you will grow. If you train hard, then you will win this race with ease. It's all about choices once again.......

Dark Night of the Soul

At some point, on your path of Enlightenment you will encounter this phenomenon.

It is quite an experience when this happens, and it arrives by surprise. There is nothing you can do to prepare for it. Being informed about it will assist to recognise the event but you cannot stop it or turn back. Your only safety net is to understand that it's happening. All that is required is observing the process. Its starts with descending into what feels like a depressive state. You feel as if your life is at an end as everything feels hopeless and pointless. These feelings become directed towards your personal circumstances and become connected to events during your life. This could be recent events or from early in life. Utter despair and hopelessness is the main theme here. I remember crashing to the floor in a heap when this happened. Tears arrived as emotions rose to meet my throat and sobbing followed. You think you are at a low, but it continues for quite some time dragging you further down. Suicidal thoughts fill your head as the hopelessness becomes overwhelming, and the crying intensifies. The emotional pain and anguish is nothing like I have ever experienced before and the need to escape is very prominent in your mind. You feel surrounded and unable to escape this pain as it continues to drag you down. It may sound like doom and gloom, but it is a good thing as it is a big step in growth. The Ego is fighting for survival as you subconsciously reach to become one with the Higher Self. This is a massive and necessary step towards your end game of Ascension. It is a comparable to detox for an addict. It is not an easy thing to get through, but you get through it and you feel a huge sense of relief. It feels like a massive burden has been lifted from you. What is in effect happening is that you Aura is mutating and during this process it needs to change frequency. This change in frequency gives the impression that the Ego dying as it is becoming redundant. Ascension, is the changing from consciously working with the Ego to consciously working with the Higher Self instead. The Ego is what we have been used to working with all these years and is the reference point or foundation. For a human to lose this foundation is like a death as there is nothing to cling to. This is the dark night, the first taste of losing the Ego and it feels as if you are dying inside. It is not a common occurrence or at least in the past it never was. Evolution was only on a physical level but today it will become common as more people take on the path of enlightenment. It is a tough experience but looking back I can see the value and it is a rite of passage in its own way. So, a necessary event. There is a lot of folklore about the process, but this is the basis. You will know when it arrives as it doesn't appear to fit within the current day-to-day life experience. Just sit back and allow it to happen.

Philippe Roels

Allow

When we allow something to happen, we relinquish control.

If we think about control, then it conjures up many aspects to many people, some good and some not so good. Control has its roots firmly planted within the construct of Ego because Ego needs validation and purpose. This gives us a sense of being worthy. It is almost impossible to see this unless you have arrived at a place where it is time for you to know this. This will become something you need to face and is part of the process of Enlightenment. Ascension is the dismantling of the Ego and replacing it with the Higher Self. It is safe to say that "Allowing" this to happen is key, and it becomes a process of observation. This path is set by your Higher self and it will happen one way or another. All you really need to do is observe this as it happens. Previously, you would not be aware of this but now as you gain in awareness these things are no longer hidden. The act of allowing is giving permission to your Higher Self. To do what, you might ask? Well, to get involved and show the way forward because by now you also realise that the Ego knows nothing. The Ego is in the survival game and wants to remain present in this dimension. The Ego is not concerned with ascension because it does not know another existence. The Ego is a product of experiencing this dimension, so it only knows this dimension. Everything that the Ego knows is learnt right here on Earth. The Ego seeks completion but does not have the tools or the consciousness level to attain it. If you want to ascend, then this will not serve you well and you need a new method of experience, new knowledge. So, as we are here and now, we need to transition to the next level without leaving this place as we do in the death process. I think now you can see where I'm going with this. The Higher Self has to become the primary source of your experience, so we need to switch over to this from Ego. To do this, we need to "ALLOW" the higher Self to show us how to do this because nobody else can advise us. It has never been done before. Even if somebody could tell you how it feels, this would make no sense because the Ego cannot grasp this.

This is the reason it becomes important to listen and allow the process to take place. We practice this and refine our understanding by engaging in Meditation and Yoga. Meditation helps us to become more sensitive to the finer energies and Yoga helps us to move these energies through the body. Meditation allows us to explore our unseen Universe and Yoga helps us to clear old energy blocked by poor circulation of energies. The channels are unused or become damaged due to stressful living. The only way to use these disciplines effectively is to take part and Allow the process to unlock these avenues or channels.

So how do we Allow? For me this all happened on the mat during a combination of Yoga and Meditation. It started with feeling the energy whilst just standing and relaxing at the start of the practice. Feeling the energy and then noticing that it wanted to move me in a certain way, not standard to a typical start of a Yoga sequence. I wanted to explore this further and delve deeper into the energy hoping to gain a greater experience and more insight. The only way I could achieve this was to make myself even more available to the process so in effect Allowing further. It sounds strange but once you do this yourself, then it will make more sense. So, I discovered that this process was just "Allowing" or giving in to this and observing. This is how I ended up with this term, but I realise that you need to experience this to find that place where this happens. It's not complicated, but it is helpful if you are given a hint on where to look. We need to turn up and let things happen because we cannot die and therefore anything else is an experience in this dimension. It's a great ride if we allow this to happen and the Universe will reveal many lovely secrets to us.

Just ALLOW. Turn up on your mat and what will be, will be.

Surrender

Allow and eventually you will arrive at Surrender.

You will be ready to surrender when you develop trust in your Higher Self. Surrender has depth, it's like the Ocean and can be explored. How deep you go is entirely up to you but If you are anything like me, then you'll endeavour to turn over each stone and look for as much as possible. Surrendering to the process of Enlightenment from my point of view guarantees I'm getting the most from the experience and allows for the earliest development possible. Personally, I have always searched for answers and yearned to explore the Universe. I guess it's a factor that drives me. To surrender is a culmination of many factors, Truth, Trust and dispelling of fear. I believe without those aspects you cannot Surrender. It's a place that can be thought of as a feeling. When you arrive at Surrender, you will know. Your Higher Self-will envelop you and you will feel safe. You will be in a place where you have so much trust in your Higher Self that you will feel ok with the idea of your higher Self removing you from this Earth.

Now you are ready! Ready for communication with the Universe and with your higher Self. You will experience events, places and people you never imagined or considered. All these experiences will provide you with insight into your Universe and you will see your place within it. You will feel a sense of belonging, a connection to other realities. This is the place of Surrender it has great depth as each discovery opens a new door to a deeper level. Allowance is a layer or like a blanket but Surrender has depth so there is lots to explore. Even now at this level there are trials as you navigate these depths your own energy continues to transform and adjust. You continue to grow and discover new levels of yourself almost daily. All the while you are becoming more in tune with all energies and not limited to this dimension. I started to notice energy bleeding through from neighbouring dimensions even energy seeping through from different timelines. For example, Déjà vu became more frequent and sensing somebody's presence or their impending arrival became the norm. Intention can be felt before any other action takes place particularly if it is directed at you in person. So how do we Surrender? How do you know if you are ready to tackle this? The simplest way I have found in describing this is to go back to "The Breath". The third and last step of the technique, the pause before the next inhale is the key. Practice this breath and in time it will develop for you. When you arrive at the end of the "Out breath", that small moment where all is quiet, feel this place just for a second. Now gently push down into the perineum, it should feel like a small trampoline flexing. This is not a physical movement of the body but picture this happening to give it strength because of your intention. Now transition gently back to the "in breath". Surrender into this pause after a while it may even feel as if the pause is getting longer or that you could even make it longer if you wish.

Awakening to Enlightenment and Ascension

Ascension

A simple way to describe the process is as follows. Imagine that you are in the middle of Ocean and miles from anywhere. All you can see is water, and you are encased in a large ball of ice. You are submerged in this ocean and surrounded by ice.

Now consider this, the ocean is your Higher Self and the ball of ice is your Soul or Aura. You can picture by the description that the density is different between the two. This difference in density is the cause of separation between you and your Higher Self. Information from the Higher Self cannot penetrate the ice due to its higher density. This is the separation or the veil that we believed to be in place. It makes us feel alone and disconnected but we never are as we are housed or contained within the greater Universe that is created by the Higher Self, the ocean. The known Universe is created by the Higher Self and is made of itself. So now we turn our attention to the ball of ice or Aura and within the ice there are patches varying in density. Some areas are so dense that they are black as no light can penetrate at all. These denser areas are in "Dis-ease" because the flow is restricted or not present. As the flow cannot permeate throughout the ice it therefore cannot get to you within the ice at its core. If you think of your Aura as the ball of ice then you can see why and how physical pain arrives in your body. It is a lack of flow or restricted flow. So, if the flow is restored then the body will once again be "At ease" and therefore free from "Dis-ease".

The ascension process starts by returning the ball of ice to its state of "Good flow" with no uneven patches of ice. This is the hard part as you need to identify the areas with lack of flow and restore it. As you work on this phase, the overall density of the ice changes and it becomes softer, reaching out to become part of the ocean once again. Once the ice melts due to the increase frequency and therefore increased energy levels, you become one with your Higher Self and are at a similar frequency for the density dimension.This is a basic example of the process, but you can see that your frequency needs to raise to a certain level before you can have free and uninterrupted communication with the Higher Self. At the moment we cannot see or hear beyond our Aura and this is the current separation. Ascension is becoming one with the Higher Self.

Awakening to Enlightenment and Ascension

Conclusion

Remember that this is only a small part in a very large experience. It's hard to put into written words but I'm planning a book with a more comprehensive account. This is just an introduction into the tools of "The System" and I realize that there will be many questions. The information you have here is enough to give you basic insight and a start point but if you have questions then get in touch. I offer a mentoring service as I realize that this is not a quick process and it can stretch out for some time. This all depends on how you progress yourself as we are all different, but It can range from two years upwards. Being keen and ready to start the work is great but does not guarantee the rate of progress. Having said that if you have read this book then you will have gained some insight. The mere fact that you took the time to get through this material is a good sign and your intention is aimed in the right direction. Keep working and continue your search. One day you will connect with your soul and you will have arrived. You will understand the Universe and your place within it. The illusion will no longer be your reality and you will have become a master. Peace will arrive, and it will be awesome.

ABOUT THE AUTHOR

Philippe had his awakening in 1994 and has been teaching Meditation since 1998. His teaching techniques encompass a variety of methods that have been successful in helping many people to progress on their path. Philippe was born in France and spent a great part of his life in South Africa. His work has taken him around the world and he now resides in the U.K. He has channelled a great deal of information about the awakening of mankind and his teachings are as a result of his personal experiences on his path of Enlightenment. Now he works on anchoring the energy of change along side his personal approaching Ascension.

Book 2 – I am not Human

A second book in this series is in production. This volume will deal with the origins of the author. Where he comes from and what his mission is about. It will highlight his journey and how he came to discover the Universal knowledge. Insight into cross dimensional knowledge and the beings that assist mankind on the path.

Dawn Bickel - 561 888 0957

Gone 8 hrs. Friday
Sat out by 1:00 - then to Airport
Cancelled Flight, To Rosies back to
System 1:00 Sunday.